COLOR THRU HISTORY

The People of the Renaissance & Reformation
Elementary Supplement

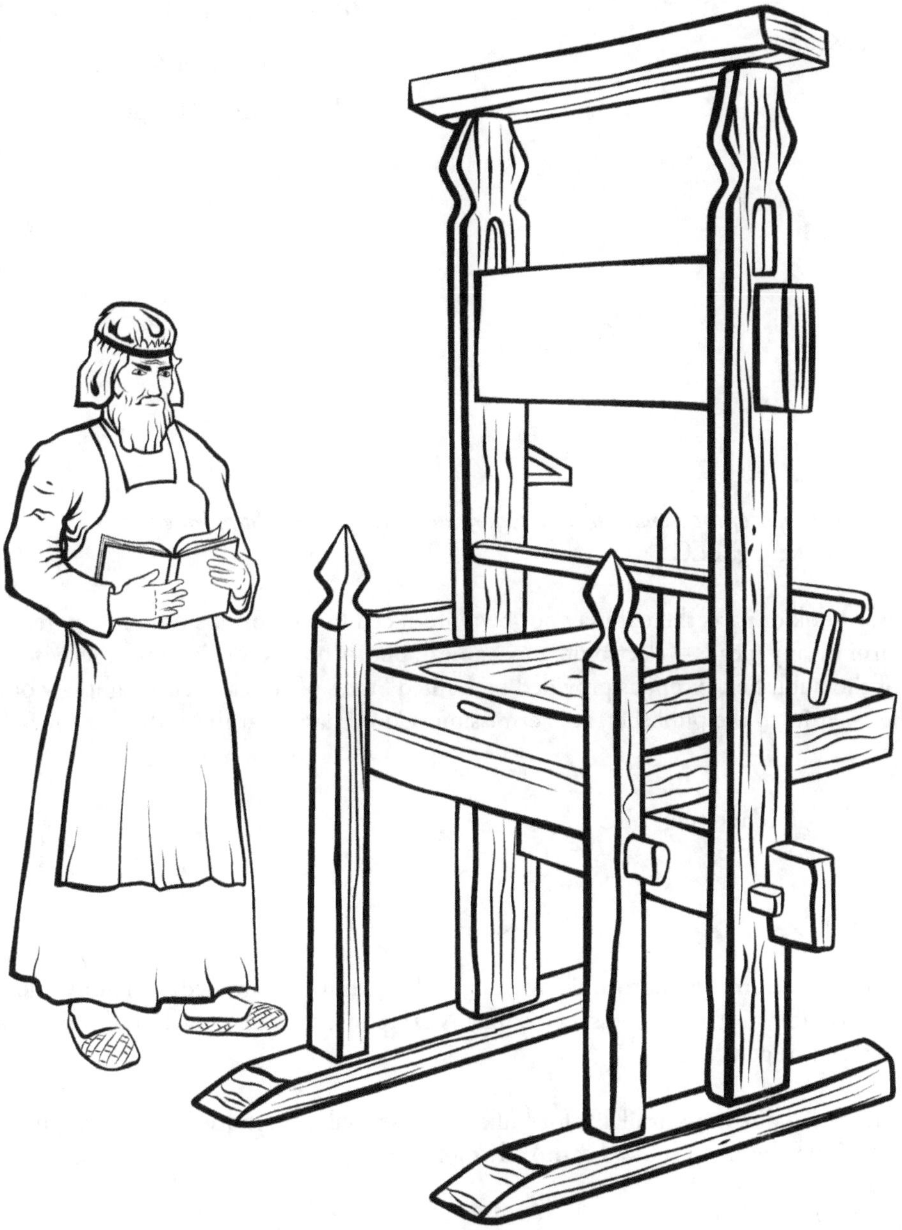

Fulton, KY

Current and upcoming titles:

Learn and Color Nature Series
- Medicinal Herbs
- Freshwater Fish
- Garden Edibles
- Reptiles

Learn and Color Stained Glass Series
- Landscapes & Seascapes
- Fish & Fowl
- Flowers

- Early Civilization
- The Ancient World
- The Middle Ages
- The Renaissance and Reformation
- The Industrial Revolution
- The Modern Age
- The Computer Age

Color Thru History™ – The People of the Renaissance & Reformation Elementary Supplement
© 2020 Master Design Marketing, LLC

All rights reserved. This book or parts thereof may not be reproduced in any form, stored in any retrieval system, or transmitted in any form by any means—electronic, mechanical, photocopy, recording, or otherwise—without prior written permission of the publisher, except as provided by United States of America copyright law or as noted below. For permission requests, write to the publisher, at "Permissions Coordinator," at the address below.

Learn & Color Books
 an imprint of Master Design Marketing, LLC
789 State Route 94 E
Fulton, KY 42041
www.LearnAndColor.com

Permission is granted to make as many photocopies as you need for your own immediate family's homeschool use. All other use is strictly prohibited. Co-ops and schools may NOT photocopy any portion of this book. Educators must purchase one book for each student.

For information about special discounts available for bulk purchases, sales promotions, fund-raising and educational needs, contact Learn & Color Books at sales@LearnAndColor.com.

ISBN: 978-1-947482-27-2
Cover and interior design by Faithe F Thomas
Research by Caitlyn F Williams
Some images are © Faithe F Thomas
All other Images © DepositPhotos.com
Text in this book is a derivative of information by Wikipedia.com, used under CC BY 4.0.
The text of this book is licensed under CC BY 4.0 by Faithe F Thomas.
Look for the Scottish Flag somewhere in each of our books.

Johannes Gutenberg was a German inventor, printer, and publisher.
His movable-type printer started the publishing revolution.
His major work was the Gutenberg Bible.

Joan of Arc was a hero of the war between France and England. She fought for the French and helped to free the town of Orléans.

Vlad Dracula was born in what is now Transylvania. He was a strong ruler, but his enemies tried to make him look bad by saying he drank blood. These tales strongly influenced stories of vampires.

The Medici family was considered the wealthiest in Europe for a time. They paid for the construction of Saint Peter Basilica and helped people like da Vinci, Michelangelo, Machiavelli, and Galileo.

Christopher Columbus was an Italian explorer, navigator, and colonist. He led the first European expeditions to the Caribbean, Central America, and South America.

Leonardo da Vinci was one of the most diversely talented individuals ever to have lived. *The Mona Lisa* is the most famous of his works of art. But he also invented many machines.

Amerigo Vespucci was an Italian explorer and map maker. He was the first one to suggest that North America was a new world. In fact, the name America comes from his first name in Latin: *Americus*.

Niccolò Machiavelli was an Italian diplomat, politician, and historian.
He has often been called the father of modern political science.
He wrote a book about a dishonest prince.

Nicolaus Copernicus was a mathematician and astronomer. He created a model of the universe that placed the Sun rather than the Earth at the center of the universe.

Juan Ponce de León was a Spanish explorer.
He led the first known European expedition to La Florida.

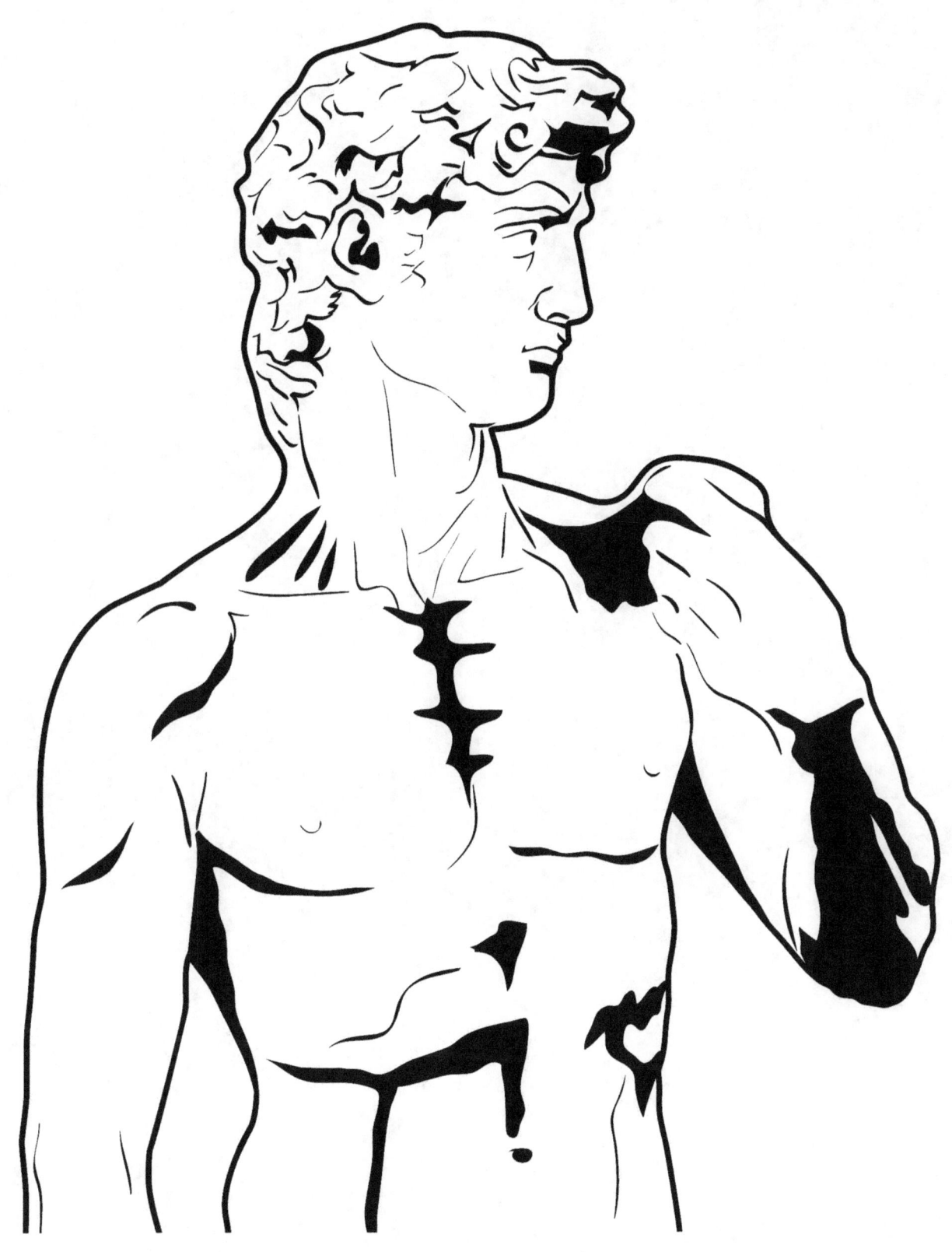

Michelangelo was an Italian sculptor, painter, architect, and poet. He sculpted the statue known as *David* before the age of thirty.

Ferdinand Magellan was a Portuguese explorer.
He nearly sailed all the way around the planet
for the first time in history.

Luther was a priest who taught that salvation was not earned by good deeds but received only as the free gift of God's grace through faith in Jesus Christ as redeemer from sin. He also translated the Bible into German.

Raphael was an Italian painter and architect.
Together with Michelangelo and Leonardo da Vinci,
he forms the traditional trinity of great masters of this period.

Jacques Cartier was a Breton explorer who claimed what is now Canada for France. He was one of the first to formally acknowledge that the New World was a separate land mass from Europe/Asia.

Suleiman the Magnificent led Ottoman armies in conquering Christian strongholds. He ruled over 15 to 25 million people.

Nostradamus was a French physician and author of the book *Les Propheties*, which supposedly predicts future events.

John Calvin was a French theologian, pastor, and reformer in Geneva during the Protestant Reformation. He developed the system of Christian theology later called Calvinism.

John Knox was a Scottish minister, theologian, and writer who was a leader of the Scottish Reformation and the founder of the Presbyterian Church of Scotland.

Ivan the Terrible was the first Tsar of Russia. He was an able diplomat, a patron of arts and trade, and the founder of Russia's first publishing house.

Sir Francis Drake was an English sea captain, privateer, slave trader, naval officer, and explorer. He was the second person to go all the way around the planet.

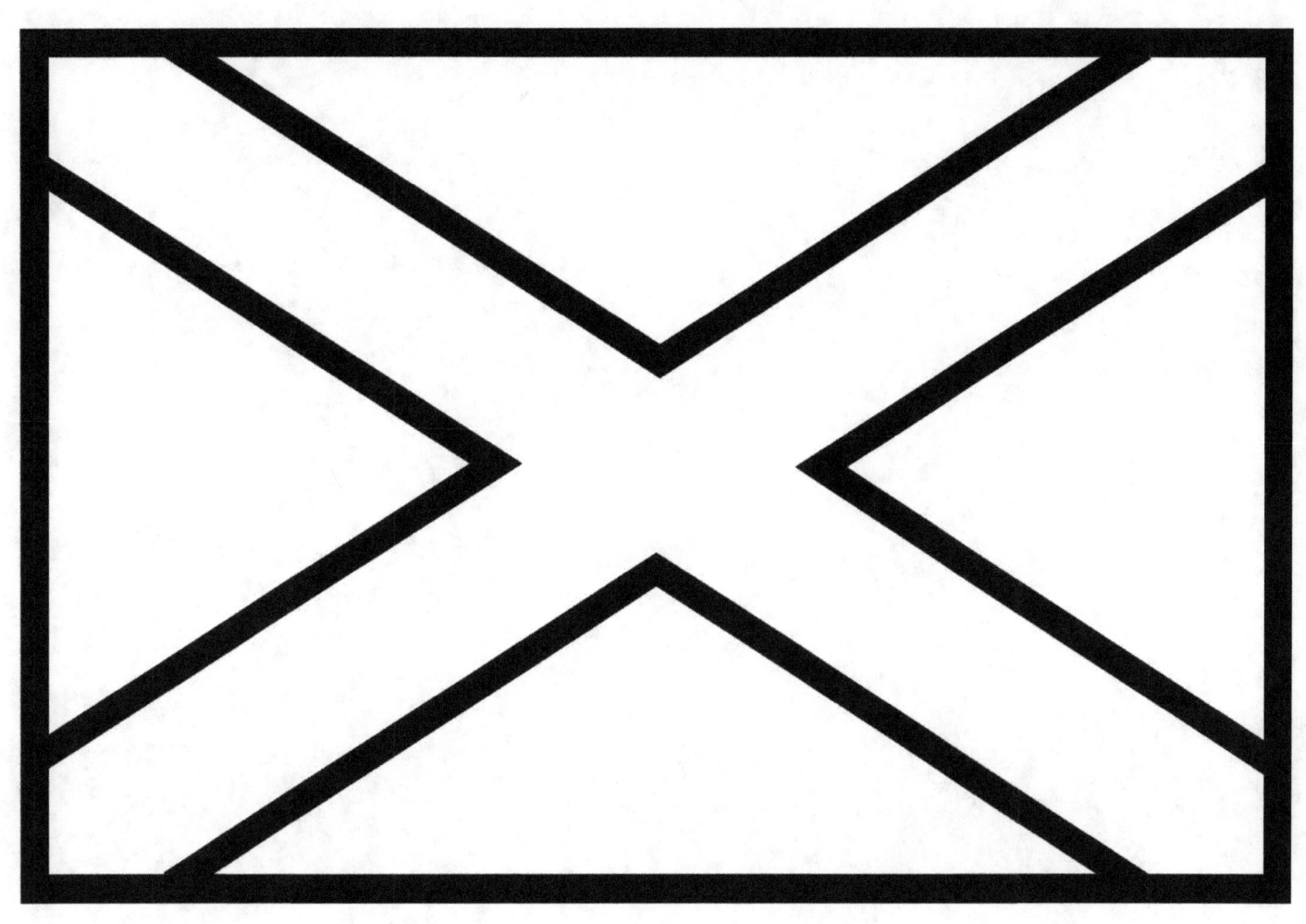

Mary, Queen of Scots, became the queen when she was only six days old.
Later, she married and had a son name James.
He became an important king of England.

Akbar was the third Mughal emperor. He ruled most of India.

Galileo Galilei was an Italian astronomer, physicist, and engineer. He has been called the Father of Astronomy, the Father of Modern Physics, the Father of the Scientific Method, and the Father of Modern Science.

William Shakespeare was an English poet, playwright, and actor.
He wrote plays like *Romeo and Juliet*.

James was King of Scotland and King of England and Ireland. He was the son of Mary, Queen of Scots. He sponsored the translation of the Bible into English that would later be named the *King James Version*.

Johannes Kepler was a German astronomer and mathematician.
He figured out the paths that planets take around the sun.

Pocahontas was the daughter of Powhatan, an Indian chief in Virginia. She married John Rolfe, which brought peace between the English and the Indians for many years.

René Descartes was a French philosopher, mathematician, and scientist.
Even today, people use his math and discoveries.

Sir Isaac Newton was an English mathematician, physicist, astronomer, theologian, and author. He is widely recognized as one of the most influential scientists of all time.

www.ingramcontent.com/pod-product-compliance
Lightning Source LLC
Chambersburg PA
CBHW081756100526
44592CB00015B/2463